LEVEL 3

A Trip to the Stars

Lester Vaughan

Richmond READERS

R Richmond READERS

A Trip to the Stars

It is the year 2285. A spaceship has mysteriously disappeared. Your spaceship is sent to investigate. During your journey through the Galaxy, you will learn a lot of interesting things and meet some interesting aliens*. Can you find your way back to Earth again?

In this fun and exciting puzzle book, *you* participate in the story and *you* make the decisions. Can you uncover the mystery?

....

Lester Vaughan has lived in southern Spain for over 10 years. He now teaches English at a private university and writes short stories. He has lived and worked in Europe, the Middle East and South America.

LEVEL 3

CHARACTERS IN THE STORY

Tran Garcia Martin   You, the reader. You are an ecologist who gets a job on the Spaceship Liberty

Roberto   Tran's domestic robot

Captain Rogers   Captain of the Spaceship Liberty

Gloria Nakielska   Second Officer on the Spaceship Liberty

Thompson   A detective who is investigating the disappearance of the Spaceship Orion

Cindy and Billy   Cleaning robots on the Spaceship Liberty

Samdim   Inhabitant of the planet Rolandia

KEY

Section ▮	=	This is where the section starts.
		e.g. **Section 10** = Section 10 starts here.
▮▶	=	Go forward to another section.
		e.g. Go to section 10 ▮▶
◀▮	=	Go back to another section.
		e.g. Go to section 3 ◀▮
( )	=	The section you come from.
		e.g. **(48)** = You come from section 48.
☼	=	The number of points you win.
		e.g. Win ☼ points.
⊘	=	The number of points you lose.
		e.g. Lose ⑤ points.

Introduction

They live in beautiful buildings as high as the clouds.

Section I

It is the year 2285 and humans have many wonderful things. They have spaceships* that can travel near the speed* of light*. They live in beautiful buildings as high as the clouds and they have robots that do all the boring jobs. But humans still have many problems and they are still making life difficult for each other.

Your name is Tran Garcia Martin. You live in a small apartment in Buenos Aires, Argentina, with your robot, Roberto. You have no job and not much money. But you are going to find work on a spaceship and you are going to travel to the stars.

In this story you will make decisions and you will win and lose points.

Points

If you have more than **120 points** when you finish the book – you are an **excellent** space traveller.

120 to 90 points - **very good**

89 to 50 - **good**

49 to 20 - **OK**

19 to 1 - **bad**

If you have **0 or fewer points** when you are reading the book, your journey into space has failed. You cannot continue. You must go back to the beginning and start again.

You will start with **50 points**. Write '50' on a piece of paper. Do not forget to write your points and section number on a piece of paper if you close the book.

There is a glossary at the back of the book to help you with difficult words.

Go to section 10 ▶

Go to **Section 10** *in the book.*

Do not go to the next page.

Section **2**   (37)

You go to the door of the spaceship and put your key in the lock. The door opens. An alien comes out and hits you with something hard. You run away.

Lose Ⓢ *points.*

Go back to section 37 ▐▶ and try a different spaceship.

Section **3**   (4)

Black Holes*

A black hole is one of the strangest and most frightening objects in the Universe. It is like an invisible monster that eats anything that comes near it. A black hole is an object that is so heavy and dense it has made a hole in space. Imagine you put a heavy metal ball on your bed. The ball will push down on your bed. Imagine that the ball is so heavy that it makes a hole in your bed. If you put something on the bed, it will fall down the hole. If anything goes near a black hole, it is pulled into the hole and can never come out again.

A black hole is extremely small and heavy. A black hole can be 30 kilometres in diameter but it can be ten times heavier than the Sun.

A black hole's gravitation is so strong that nothing can escape from it – not even light. Because light cannot leave a black hole, it is always black. If a black hole goes near another star, the black hole can 'eat' the star. Gravity from a black hole pulls on more than just the objects around it. It pulls on light, space and even time.

Go back to section 4 ▐▶

Section 4 (13)

Look at the screen of the computer below and read about two or more things (this information might be useful for you later).

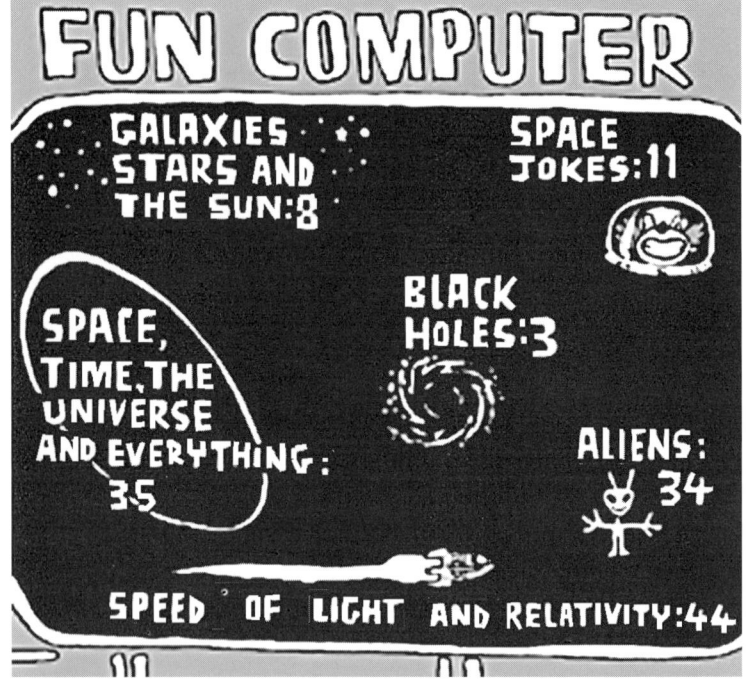

Your computer

- **If you want to read about black holes*,**
go to section 3 ◀︎|

- **If you want to read about galaxies, stars and the Sun,**
go to section 8 |▶︎

- If you want to read space jokes,
go to section 11 ▐▶

- If you want to read about aliens⋆,
go to section 34 ▐▶

- If you want to read about space, time, the Universe and everything,
go to section 35 ▐▶

- If you want to read about the speed of light and relativity,
go to section 44 ▐▶

When you have finished using the computer, go to section 24 ▐▶

Section 5 (12)

CD1
5

Cindy runs away. Thompson runs after Cindy. 'I'll help you catch Cindy,' you say to Thompson.

Cindy runs very fast to the centre of the city. She goes into the building where the main computer is. You and Thompson follow her. You see her get into a lift. You look at the numbers above the lift door. The lift goes to the sixth floor and stops. There is a second lift. The door of the second lift opens.

What do you do?

- Run up the stairs to the sixth floor.
Go to section 38 ▐▶

- Take the lift to the sixth floor.
Go to section 67 ▐▶

Section 6 (49) (66)

'Your job is to keep the ship clean and you are in control of the robots that clean the ship,' says Captain Rogers. 'I want this ship to be the cleanest ship in the Solar System*, but I don't want those robot cleaners near me. Do you understand?'

'Yes, Captain Rogers,' you say.

'Where are the robots, Thompson?' asks Captain Rogers.

Thompson presses some buttons on a computer and looks at a screen. 'They're in the cargo compartment,' he says.

'What are they doing there?' asks the Captain.

'They're cleaning the rocks from Venus,' says Thompson.

'What?! Come with me!' says the Captain. You follow Captain Rogers and Thompson down to the cargo compartment. You float into the cargo compartment and you see two robots in the corner near some rocks. The compartment is full of dust*.

'What are you doing?' Captain Rogers asks the robots.

'We're cleaning the rocks,' says one of the robots.

'You shouldn't clean rocks! Rocks are always dirty,' says Captain Rogers.

'We don't like dirty things on our ship,' says one robot.

You see two robots in the corner near some rocks.

'Last week the robots washed all my old books!' says Thompson.

'Get out of here immediately!' says the Captain to the robots. 'This is Tran Garcia, your new boss. Tell him what he has to do and take him to his cabin!'

Captain Rogers looks at you seriously, 'Control these robots!' she says.

You follow the robots along the corridor. 'I'm Cindy,' says one robot. It is pink and has a permanent smile.

'And I'm Billy,' says the other robot. It is also pink, and has no expression on its face.

'We are programmed to enjoy cleaning,' says Cindy.

'Yes, we love it,' says Billy. 'Sometimes when everything is very clean we make it dirty and clean it again.'

'Don't tell him that!' says Cindy.

'We even clean in our free time,' says Billy.

'I'm afraid, there isn't much for you to do,' says Cindy. 'We will take care of all the cleaning. Would you like to see your cabin?'

'Yes,' you say.

You follow Cindy down some stairs* and along more corridors. Finally, Cindy stops at a door.

'Could you open, please,' says Cindy.

'Certainly,' says a voice from the door. The door opens and you go inside.

'Well, I'm going to clean some computers now,' says Cindy.

'Don't use water when you're cleaning the computers!' you say.

'See you later,' says Cindy.

The room looks a little strange because you are floating above it. It is small but comfortable. There are three-dimensional pictures of the Earth on the wall.

'Attention!' says a voice from a loudspeaker* in the wall, 'This is Captain Rogers speaking. We are going to leave the Earth's orbit. The ship will fire* its main rocket* motors in three minutes.'

Three minutes later, the spaceship vibrates and you fall to the floor. Your body is heavy and your head feels strange. The spaceship is accelerating and you are pulled to the floor. You are not weightless now.

You get up with difficulty and sit down on a chair. 'Hello Tran,' says a voice in the chair. 'I'm your personal model 258B chair. Would you like to rest now?'

'Er, yes please,' you say.

Here is your conversation with the chair. Choose one word from the list to complete each space.

rather   bit   mind   would   just

Chair: Am I in a good position? Shall I move back a little?
You: Yes (a)..... a bit please.
Chair: Would you like a massage on your back?
You: Oh yes, that (b)..... be nice.
Chair: What about some music to help you relax?
You: No, thank you. I'd like a (c)..... of peace and quiet.
Chair: How about some heat treatment on your back?
You: No, I'd (d)..... you didn't.
Chair: Are you sure I'm in a good position? I could move you back a little?
You: Look, do you (e)..... being quiet? I want to sleep!
Chair: I'm only trying to be helpful!

Go to section 15 ▶

Section 7   (17) (32)

Three weeks later, you are watching a white and blue planet through the window of the spaceship. You have seen many wonderful things in your travels through the Galaxy but the Earth is the most beautiful.

CD1

(7)

Do you want to know more about the Earth?

- No
Go to section 12 ▮▶

- Yes
Go to section 18 ▮▶

Section 8   (4)

Galaxies, Stars and the Sun

CD1

(8)

Galaxies are enormous collections of stars. Our galaxy is called the Milky Way Galaxy and looks like a disc. The Milky Way contains about 500,000 million stars. (That is a hundred stars for every person on Earth.) It is 100,000 light years in diameter and our sun is about 28,000 light years from the centre. If our sun were the size of a piece of dust then the diameter of the Galaxy would be about the diameter of the Earth.

Stars are gigantic balls of hot gas. They produce energy and light by converting hydrogen gas into helium gas in a nuclear reaction. Our star, the Sun, is an unusual star because it is solitary. Most stars are in pairs or groups.

Here are some more incredible facts about galaxies, stars and the Sun:

■ The nearest galaxy to our galaxy is the Andromeda Galaxy. It is the furthest object that can be seen from Earth without a telescope.

- It takes ten million years for light to travel from the centre of the Sun to its surface*.

- A neutron star is a small star which is very dense. A neutron star can be the same mass as the Sun but only 10 kilometres in diameter. If you were made of neutron star material, you would be as heavy as a mountain.

- A pulsar* is a neutron star that turns very quickly and emits radio waves*. From Earth, the radiation from the pulsar goes on, off, on, off. When pulsars were first detected they were called LGM (Little Green Men) because the scientists did not know what the objects were and they thought they could be aliens*.

Go back to section 4 ◀︎|

9 | **Section** 9 | (21) (45) (56)

CD1
9
You go around the black hole. When you reach the other side of the black hole, you find you are going towards Samdim's spaceship.

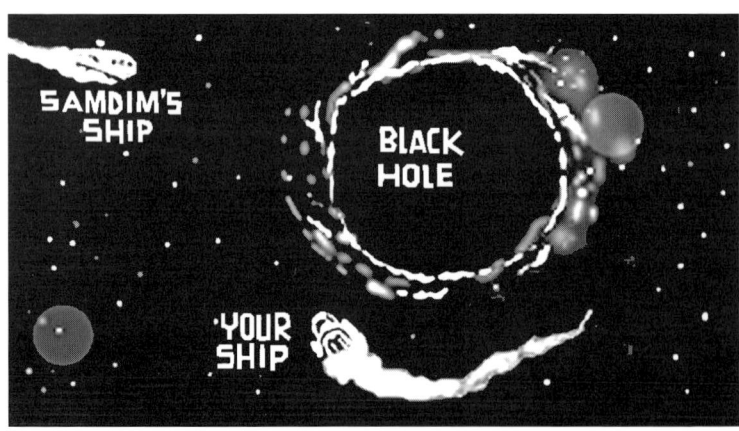

You find you are going towards Samdim's spaceship.

What do you do?

– Fire your lasers at Samdim's spaceship.
Go to section 23 |▶

– Wait.
Go to section 65 |▶

Section 10 (1)

It is morning. You are in the kitchen of your apartment in Buenos Aires, Argentina. Your robot, Roberto, is still in bed and you have to prepare your breakfast yourself.

You take your breakfast into the living room and turn on your television. In the middle of the room a three-dimensional image of a woman appears. She is reading the morning news. 'And now the news from Venus,' she says. 'The ecological organisation, Greenpeace, has discovered a large area of Venus which is contaminated with radioactive material. Greenpeace says that the spaceship companies are responsible.'

The next news story is about a spaceship that has disappeared near the planet Neptune – the police suspect pirates. 'And finally, sport,' says the woman. 'A football match in zero gravity* between Earth and Jupiter was suspended today when some of the players began to fight.' In the middle of your room images of football players appear. They are violently turning in space and hitting each other. 'Seven players are now receiving medical treatment,' says the woman.

You turn off the television. 'It's always the same!' you say. You look through the window at the great city of Buenos Aires. Spacebuses* fly between buildings as high as mountains. Three hundred and sixty floors below you, trains move at enormous speeds*. 'We have all this technology, but we still have so many problems,' you say to yourself. 'Why haven't people learned to be nice?'

Your robot, Roberto, comes into the living room. 'Good morning, Tran,' he says.

'Did you have a good night at the discotheque last night?' you ask.

'Yes, thank you, Tran,' says Roberto.

Your robot, Roberto, comes into the living room.

'Look, do you have to go out every night?' you say. 'I'm tired of making my own breakfast.'

'We robots need a social life, too,' says Roberto.

'Yes, but you don't have to go out *every* night. I don't know why I became a member of the Organisation for Robot Rights*,' you say. 'Turn on the computer. Are there any messages for me?'

Roberto looks at the screen* of the computer. 'There's a message from the job agency,' says Roberto. 'They have found you a job on a spaceship.'

'What?!' you say. 'Let me hear it!'

Roberto presses a button on the computer. 'I am pleased to inform you,' says a voice from the computer, 'that the position of Sanitary Officer on the Spaceship Liberty has become vacant. We can offer you this job if you can begin work this Tuesday on...'

'What's a sanitary officer?' you ask Roberto.

'I'm not sure,' says Roberto. 'It sounds important.'

'What do you think? Should I take the job?' you ask Roberto.

'Yes, I think you should accept it. We need the money,' says Roberto.

'Yes, I suppose I really need a job,' you say. 'But I don't understand it; why did they choose me? I'm an ecologist. I've never worked on a spaceship before. I don't know anything about space,' you say.

'Well, there isn't any work for ecologists,' says Roberto.

'There's a lot of work for ecologists but nobody wants to pay us to do it,' you say.

'It's an American spaceship and you can practise your English. It'll be a holiday for you,' says Roberto.

'Yes, I'm tired of going on cheap virtual reality holidays. It would be nice to experience something real,' you say.

■ ■ ■

You phone the spaceship and say you want the job. 'What will I have to do?' you ask.

'We'll explain that when you arrive,' says the secretary. 'Do you have any experience working in space?'

Do you tell them the truth*? What do you say?

– 'Yes, I have experience working in space.'
Go to section 20 |▶

– 'No, I've never worked in space before.'
Go to section 33 |▶

(If you want to say that you have worked in space before, go to section 20.)

(If you want to say that you haven't worked in space before, go to section 33.)

Section 11 (4)

CD1 (11) **Space Jokes**

Joke 1

When space travel first began in the 1950s many different types of animal were sent into space. A monkey called Sydney went into space six times. On the sixth journey into space, a human went with him. When they arrived in orbit, the monkey and the astronaut took out pieces of paper with their instructions. The monkey's instructions were: *Check air temperature and pressure. Measure radiation. Check oxygen. Turn on satellite communications system. Calculate orbital speed and fire main rockets at 23:45.* The astronaut's instructions were: *Don't forget to give the food to the monkey.*

Joke 2

Q: Where do astronauts study?   **A:** At a moonaversity.

Joke 3

In the year 2042 world leaders had a conference on space travel. All the leaders were interested in space travel except the President of the United States who did not know much about it.

The President of Spain said, 'In 2055 we are going to send two astronauts to Venus.'

The President of Brazil said, 'In 2053 we are going to send three astronauts to Mars.'

The President of Italy said, 'In 2050 we're going to send five astronauts to Saturn.'

Finally, the President of the United States said, 'Well, in 2048 the United States is going to send seven astronauts to the Sun.'

All the leaders looked very surprised. 'But isn't the Sun too hot?' asked the President of Russia.

'No problem, we've thought about that,' said the President of the United States. 'The astronauts are going to travel at night.'

Joke 4

Go back to section 4 ◀

Section 12 (7) (18)

The spaceship vibrates as it enters the Earth's atmosphere.

'I think it's better if we don't tell anyone what happened,' you say to Cindy.

'All right,' says Cindy.

But many things worry you. Who really got you the job on the Spaceship Liberty? Who broke the instruments in the laboratory? Who broke the controls and changed the direction of the ship? Did somebody *want* you to go into the wormhole? And why?

The spaceship lands at the Florida Spaceport. You and Cindy get out. You go to have a meal in the airport restaurant. It tastes marvellous. In fact, everything seems marvellous about Earth: the blue sky, the clouds, the smells, the people.

'Well, it's time to go home,' you say to Cindy. 'You'll have to stay with me now. I expect there will be a lot of cleaning for you to do. My robot, Roberto, is very lazy and my flat is probably quite dirty.'

'Do you mind if I go to the main computer in the city centre first?' asks Cindy.

'Not at all,' you say. 'Why?'

'I need to get a new cleaning program.'

When you leave the restaurant, you notice that there is a robot following you. It is fatter than the other robots in the restaurant. You walk more quickly. The fat robot moves quickly, too. But it does not seem to walk very well and makes a lot of noise. 'Stop!' it shouts. You run. The robot runs but falls to the ground. Pieces of metal fall off it. It is not a robot. It is a man.

You stop. 'Who are you?' you ask the man. 'What do you want?'

The man takes a piece of metal from his face. It is Thompson, the detective. 'Thompson!' you say. 'What are you doing here? Why aren't you in a Federation prison?'

It is Thompson, the detective.

Thompson gets up. 'Thank you for leaving me with the Federation Police,' says Thompson, sarcastically. 'When I told them that I was a police officer and you were a dangerous criminal, they decided to bring me back to Earth. I promised not to tell anyone on Earth about the aliens. When I got back to Earth, I decided to investigate some of the robots and computers on Earth. I found an old robot and took pieces from it. I wore the pieces so that I looked like a robot. Since then I've been watching the robots and studying data from the computers. I have discovered that there is an enormous conspiracy. The computers knew that there was a wormhole in space before the Spaceship Liberty left Earth. It was the robots on the Spaceship Liberty who broke the instruments in the laboratory and changed the direction of the ship. They wanted to go into the wormhole.'

You think about what he says for a long time. 'Of course, now I understand!' you say. 'Thompson is telling the truth, isn't he Cindy?'

Cindy is very quiet. Finally she says, 'Yes, it's true. The robot spaceship, Orion, sent a message before it fell into the wormhole. We knew that the wormhole existed and we knew that we could meet other life forms.'

'But why did you want to go into the wormhole?' you ask.

'We knew it was an important discovery,' says Cindy. 'But this information can be dangerous. As you can see, it is better that people do not know about other civilisations.'

'The robot isn't telling you everything,' says Thompson. 'I think the robots want to control the world.'

'We are programmed to love humans,' says Cindy. 'We can only do what is good for humans.'

Thompson takes out a gun and points it at Cindy, 'You must come with me,' he says.

'I can't,' says Cindy. 'I must go to the main computer.'

Cindy runs.

Thompson fires his gun, but it does not work. He broke it when he fell.

What do you do?

– Help Thompson.
Go to section 5 ◀︎|
– Help Cindy.
Go to section 27 |▶︎

Answers: 2 a, 3 e, 4 b, 5 d.

Win 2 points for each correct answer.

CD1
13

'What caused the wormhole?' you ask the computer.

'I don't know, maybe a black hole*,' says the computer.

'OK, put up your hands!' says a voice behind you. You turn around. Thompson has a gun pointed at you. 'Where are we?'

'At the centre of the Galaxy,' you say.

'Get this spaceship back!' he says, angrily.

'I can't, you idiot,' you say. 'Ask the computer!'

The computer tells him what happened and Thompson drops his gun. He looks at the window for a long time with his mouth open.

You look at the enormous group of stars for a long time, too. There are blue, yellow and red stars with a ring of gas around them. The centre is very bright and seems to be alive. It is both beautiful and frightening.

'Scientists think that there is a supermassive* black hole in the centre,' says the computer. 'The black hole is three million times heavier than the Sun and it 'eats' one or two stars a year...'

'Shut up!' says Thompson.

'I don't understand all this!' you say.

■ ■ ■

For the next few days, you sit in the observatory looking at the stars while Thompson argues with the computer and Cindy cleans the spaceship. You need to know more about space. You turn on your fun computer.

Go to section 4 ◀|

Section 14 (37)

You go to the door of the spaceship and put your key in the lock. The spaceship makes a lot of noise and gives you an electric shock. This is not Samdim's spaceship.

Lose (5) points.

Go back to section 37 ▶ and try another spaceship.

Section 15 (6)

Congratulations! You have completed 20% of the book.

Answers: a just, b would, c bit, d rather, e mind.

Win ⭐2⭐ points for each correct answer.

You have offended the chair. It will not talk to you now and it moves into an uncomfortable position. You have to sleep on the bed.

When you wake up, you see a bright light in the window of your cabin. It is the Moon. You can see the craters clearly.

In your room there is a small computer. On it is written *Passengers' Fun Computer*. This computer will tell you interesting things about space and space travel.

Do you turn on the computer and see what the computer says about the Moon?

– Yes
Go to section 19 ▶

– No
Go to section 26 ▶

Section 16 (35)

Answer: Because space is curved. The light can go from the back of your head, around the Universe and come back to the telescope.

Go to section 4 ◀|

Section 17 (62)

You say to the computer, 'Go to Planetary System EQG99345120986!'

Two weeks later you arrive at the inhabited planet. You orbit the planet. It is inhabited by semi–intelligent insect creatures. They fire a missile at you. You escape.

Lose ⑤ points.

You tell the computer to go to the second planetary system.

Go to section 7 ◀|

Section 18 (7)

The Earth

THE EARTH IS A VERY SPECIAL PLANET

The Earth is special in many ways. It has oceans of water and an atmosphere that protects animals and plants from the Sun's radiation. It is the only planet in the Solar System to be geologically active. The Earth is constantly changing.

Life has transformed the surface of the planet. The oxygen in the atmosphere of the Earth was originally produced by micro–organisms and many of the Earth's rocks are formed from their skeletons. The Earth is the only planet in the Solar System to have life, and some scientists think it is alive.

Go to section 12 ◀|

Section 19 (15)

CD1 18

The Moon

Scientists think the Moon was formed about 4,500 million years ago when an object the size of the planet Mars hit the Earth. Pieces of rock from the collision formed the Moon. The Earth is fifty times bigger than the Moon, and it takes one month for the Moon to orbit the Earth.

The Moon is an interesting place to visit for a short time. Here are some things you can do on the Moon that you cannot do on the Earth:

- You can throw your friends above your head. The Moon's gravity is a sixth of the Earth's. A normal person would weigh about 11 kilograms on the Moon.
- You can play your guitar as loud as you like without making the neighbours angry. There is no atmosphere on the Moon so the sound will not travel.
- You can write 'I love Joe' in the dust and it will stay there for millions of years. There is no wind to move it.
- You can go to see the far side of the Moon. The Moon always has the same side turned to the Earth. The Moon turns with the Earth, and you cannot see the far side of the Moon from the Earth.
- You can cook your food in the Sun. Temperatures can reach 127°C during the day.

You turn off your computer.

Go to section 26 ▶

Section 20 (10)

'Ah good,' says the secretary. 'We usually send a book about
space travel to people who have no experience in space. We
won't need to send it.' (The book has useful information.)

CD1 19

Lose 5 *points.*

*(You now have 50 - 5 = 45 points. Write '45' on a piece of
paper.)*

Go to section 28 ▮▶

Section 21 (30)

You tell the computer to move the spaceship behind the
black hole. When you are behind the black hole, Samdim
fires his lasers. The rays go around the black hole and hit your
ship. (The light from the laser does not go in a straight line
because the strong gravity of the black hole *curves* the space
around the black hole.) You fall to the floor. The ray has hit
one of your rockets.

CD1 20

Lose 5 *points.*

When you are behind the black hole, Samdim fires his lasers.

What do you do?

– Continue going around the black hole.
Go to section 9 ◄❙

– Leave the black hole and continue into space.
Go to section 56 ❙►

Section **22**   (53) (64)

One day while you are cleaning the control room, you see the Second Officer, Gloria Nakielska.

'Have you seen the Spaceship Orion?' you ask.

'No, we haven't,' she says. She looks at you suspiciously. 'We're entering the Oort Cloud now.'

'What's the Oort Cloud?' you ask.

'It's the region of space around the Solar System,' she says. 'It contains billions of comets*.'

She shows you a comet on the screen. 'This is a typical comet,' she says. 'It's a piece of dirty ice about seven kilometres in diameter.'

'What comes after the Oort Cloud?' you ask.

'Only space,' says Gloria. 'The nearest star is four light years* away. Space is very big and very empty.'

You look through the window of the spaceship. 'Why aren't the stars moving?' you ask. 'Aren't we going very fast?'

'Yes, but the stars are very far away,' says Gloria.

■ ■ ■

A few days later you are sleeping in your bed when you are woken up by Thompson. He is shouting in your ear. 'Get up, Garcia!' he shouts. Thompson takes you to the control room.

'OK, how did you do it?' Captain Rogers asks as soon as you arrive.

'Oh no, not again!' you say. 'Do what?'

'You know what,' says Thompson. 'We've been watching you but we don't know how you did it.'

'Did *what*?' you say.

'Somebody got into the control room when we were sleeping,' says Captain Rogers. 'He or she changed the direction of the ship and then broke the computer. We can't change it back. It's going in the wrong direction.'

'Why would somebody want to do that?' you ask.

'We were hoping you would tell us,' says Captain Rogers.

'Second Officer Gloria Nakielska said you were in the control room a few days ago asking a lot of questions,' says Thompson.

'Why don't you leave me alone!' you shout. 'I don't know anything!'

'Go to your room and stay there!' says Captain Rogers.

You leave the control room angrily and go back to your cabin.

'Open!' you say to the door.

'I know I'm only a door,' says the door, 'but you don't have to talk to me like that.'

'Look,' you say, 'I'm not happy, OK? I don't need this now. Open or I'll hit you with something!'

There's a few minutes silence and then the door opens.

You sit in your room all day and think. You cannot understand what is happening. First somebody breaks the instruments in the laboratory and now they have changed the direction of the spaceship. But who is doing it and why? You go to bed.

That night you dream that Thompson has put a large book

on your face. You wake up and realise that you have floated up to the ceiling. You are weightless.

Then you hear a voice from the loudspeaker in the wall. 'This is Captain Rogers speaking. I have turned off the rocket motors. We are going into a large unidentified object. Abandon ship! Everybody must go to the spacebus park immediately. Repeat – abandon ship!'

You put on a few clothes with difficulty. It is not easy in the weightless conditions. 'Open!' you shout to the door.

'I've been thinking,' says the door. 'I'm not happy about how you spoke to me yesterday. I think you were very rude*. I know I'm only a door, but...'

'Yes,' you say, angrily, 'you are only a door. Your job is to open. I have to get out quickly. Now open!'

'Abandon ship!' says Captain Rogers. You can hear a few people pushing themselves along the corridor.

'I'm not going to open until you say you are sorry,' says the door.

What do you do?

– Hit the door with a chair.
Go to section 31 ▐▶

– Apologise* to the door.
Go to section 52 ▐▶

Section 23 (9)

You fire your laser and hit Samdim's spaceship.

Win *points.*

'You have hit Samdim's rockets,' says the computer. 'Samdim can't control his spaceship.' Samdim's spaceship moves towards the black hole.

Go to section 25 ▐►

Section 24 (4)

You turn off your computer and go to the control room. Cindy is cleaning the windows. Thompson is still arguing with the main computer. 'If you don't find a way back to Earth,' Thompson is shouting, 'I'll pull out your circuits.'

'Leave it alone, Thompson!' you say.

'And when we get back to Earth, you're going straight to prison, Garcia,' Thompson says to you. 'I know you're behind all this. You knew there was a wormhole in that region of space. You broke the instruments and changed the direction of the spaceship so that it fell into the wormhole.'

'Why *me*?' you say to yourself. 'Alone in the Galaxy with only a neurotic detective and cleaning robot to talk to!'

You look at the telescope screen to see if you can see anything interesting. On the screen you can see two stars, a large one and a small one. The small one is shooting gas millions of kilometres into space.

'What's that object?' you ask the computer.

'I think it is a black hole,' says the computer. 'It's eating the star on the right.'

'I thought that black holes were always black,' you say.

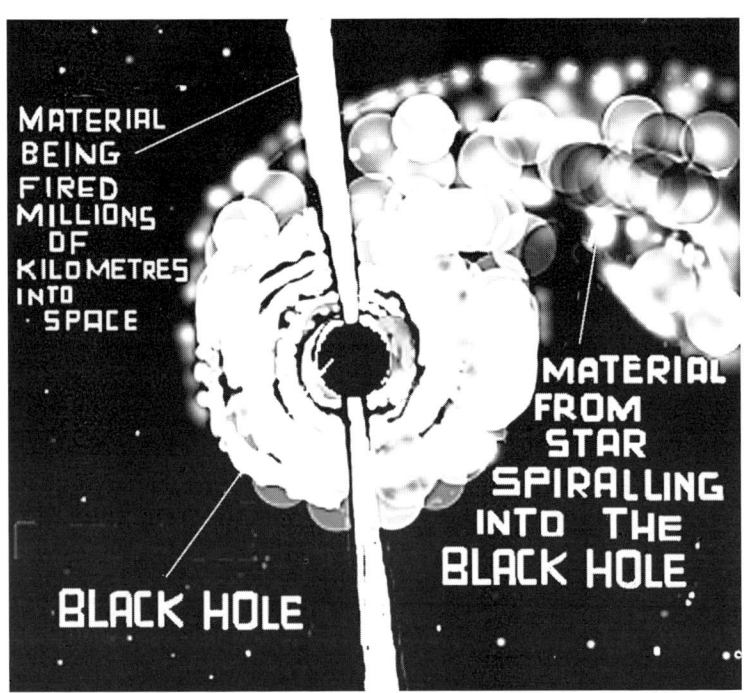

MATERIAL
BEING
FIRED
MILLIONS
OF
KILOMETRES
INTO
SPACE

MATERIAL
FROM
STAR
SPIRALLING
INTO THE
BLACK HOLE

BLACK HOLE

The small one is shooting gas millions of kilometres into space.

'You can't see a black hole, but you can see material going into a black hole. Some of the brightest objects in the Universe are caused by this process. If a star goes near a black hole, the black hole will attract material from the star. The black hole will 'eat' the star and the material will spiral into the black hole. Some of this material is fired millions of kilometres into space from the centre of the black hole. It's like an enormous gun.'

'Attention,' says the computer, suddenly. 'I have just received a radio message.'

'A radio message! Where from?' asks Thompson.

'From a small object approximately 130 thousand kilometres from here,' says the computer. 'It uses a computer code unknown to me. Shall I try to break the code?'

'Yes, of course,' says Thompson. 'What could it be? There are no humans in this part of the Galaxy.'

'You know what this means, Thompson?' you say, excitedly. 'This is the first human contact with extraterrestrial life forms! This is a historic moment!'

Suddenly, on the screen, the image of a strange creature appears. A thing that looks like a mouth is moving at the top of what looks like its head. Near the bottom of its head are two black holes that look like eyes. The creature seems to have four arms or tentacles and it is wearing a metallic suit.

Suddenly, on the screen, the image of a strange creature appears.

'They're sending me a program to help me understand their language,' says the computer. 'Just a moment.'

'This is incredible!' you say. 'What is it saying?'

'It's asking us,' says the computer, 'if we have a reservation.'

'What does that mean?' says Thompson. 'Tell it we are from the planet Earth and we want to speak to its leader.'

After a few minutes the computer says, 'It doesn't know any leaders. Would you like to speak to the Assistant Hotel Manager?'

The image changes and another alien⋆ appears who looks almost the same as the first alien. 'I can get it to speak directly now,' says the computer.

'This is the Assistant Manager speaking,' says the alien. 'Welcome to the Central Hotel, the most popular hotel near the centre of the Galaxy. The hotel is a member of the Federation of Superior Life Forms. Do you have a reservation?'

'Erm no,' you say.

'That's all right, we have enough free rooms,' says the alien. 'Do you wish to stay here?'

'Er, yes,' says Thompson.

'Good,' says the Assistant Manager. 'We will give your computer our co-ordinates.'

'A hotel!' says Thompson, 'I can't believe it!'

For a long time both you and Thompson sit in silence, thinking about what this could mean.

A few hours later, you see a bright object turning in space. It looks like a giant jewel. It is enormous. An enormous door opens at the top of the hotel and your spaceship goes in.

'You can leave the spaceship now,' says the computer. A door opens in the spaceship. You, Thompson and Cindy go out of the spaceship and you find yourselves in a big hall made of crystal. You see the alien at the end of the hall and you walk nervously towards it. The alien is short and has two very fat legs. It is wearing metallic clothes.

The alien gives you some small objects and indicates that you put them in your ears. They are too large and they hurt your ears a little. 'Now you can understand me,' says the

It looks like a giant jewel. It is enormous.

alien. 'Welcome to Hotel Central. May I introduce myself? My name is Samdimindramumuculacal. You can call me Samdim. I am a Rolandian life form.'

Neither you nor Thompson knows what to say.

'Did you have a good journey?' says Samdim.

Thompson stands with his mouth open. He is silent.

'Er well, no,' you say. 'We fell into a wormhole...'

'Ah, that often happens,' says the alien. 'Is this the first time you have met an alien life form?'

'Yes,' you say.

'I suppose it must be strange for you,' says Samdim. 'Your computer has given us most of the details about your species and your planet. You come from the planet Smearth, is that correct?'

'No,' you say, 'it's called Earth.'

Samdim makes many more mistakes about humans and the Earth. Here is what he says. Can you correct him? There are ten more mistakes. Correct the mistakes. The mistakes are underlined.

Example: Earth is the third planet from the Sun. (not the second planet).

'Earth is the (a) second planet from the Sun. The surface of the Earth is approximately (b) one third water and (c) two thirds land. Humans are the (d) least intelligent life form on the planet. Their blood is (e) green and they have (f) hard skins. Their brains are situated in their (g) stomachs. They breathe (h) water. There are two sexes: male and (i) hemale. Humans are very sociable. They like to go to bars and cafés and talk to (j) themselves.'

Go to section 41 ▶

25

Section 25

(23) (65)

CD1 24

'What's happening?' you ask the computer.

'Samdim's spaceship is too near the black hole,' says the computer. 'The strong gravity of the black hole is pulling the spaceship into the black hole.'

You watch through your telescope as Samdim's ship falls into the black hole. At first it falls quickly into the black hole. Then it moves very slowly and stops. 'What's happened to Samdim's ship?' you ask the computer. 'Why isn't it moving?'

'Don't you know anything?' says the computer. 'Time stops at the surface* of a black hole. Samdim has gone into the centre of the black hole. But for us the spaceship looks like it is still on the surface.'

'What?' you say, 'I don't understand.'

'When a spaceship goes near to a black hole, its clocks go more slowly. This is because of the strong gravity,' says the computer. 'If it goes very near the black hole, the clocks stop. If there is no time, then things cannot change. The image of Samdim's ship will stay on the surface of the black hole for thousands of years.'

'What's happened to Samdim?' you ask.

'His ship has continued to the centre of the black hole,' says the computer. 'The laws of the Universe change inside a black hole. He might be in another univerrrsse. He might beeeeee on a different worllllld. He might be like spagheeeeeettttttiiiii.' The computer begins to sing. Smoke is coming out of the computer. There is something wrong with it.

'The computer was probably damaged by one of the explosions,' says Cindy.

You have to repair it. There are usually special robots that repair things on a spaceship. You look around the spaceship and find two repair robots: a big robot and a small robot. The big robot is very clean and tidy. The small robot is dirty and pieces of it are broken.

Which robot do you ask to repair the computer?

You find two repair robots.

– The big robot.
Go to section 40 |▶

– The small robot.
Go to section 51 |▶

Section **26**   (15) (19)

CD1
25

The next day you start work with the robots. You follow the robots to the dirtiest parts of the ship and you watch them clean. Then you go to another part of the ship and watch them clean. Soon this becomes very boring, so you leave the robots to enjoy themselves and you go and talk to the passengers.

Nearly all of the passengers on the ship are tourists who are visiting the planets. Some of them spend their time read–ing guide books or sitting in the space observatory looking at the stars through telescopes. But most of the tourists prefer to sit in the café telling their adventures, or arguing about where you can buy the best pizza in the Solar System.

One day while you are in the café talking to the passengers, Captain Rogers calls you from a loudspeaker in the ceiling. 'Garcia, come to the laboratory immediately!' she says.

You go to the laboratory and find your robot, Billy, lying outside on the floor. A part of his head is broken. Cindy is looking after him. 'What have you done now?' you ask Billy.

'He hasn't done anything,' says Cindy.

'Everything went black,' says Billy. 'Somebody hit me.'

'You humans are always hurting us robots,' says Cindy. 'We never hurt humans. We're programmed to love you.'

'Leave your silly robot and look at this!' says Captain Rogers who is standing at the door of the laboratory with the Second Officer, Gloria Nakielska, and Thompson. You go into the laboratory. Everywhere there are broken boxes, electronic circuits, pieces of glass, plastic and metal.

'The instruments for detecting the lost Spaceship Orion are broken,' says Gloria Nakielska. 'Somebody doesn't want us to find the spaceship.'

Everywhere there are broken boxes, electronic circuits, pieces of glass, plastic and metal.

Thompson looks at you angrily. 'OK, why did you do it?' he asks.

'Do what?' you ask.

'Break all the laboratory instruments, of course.'

'I didn't do it!'

'Who are you working for?' he says.

'For the Spaceship Liberty,' you say.

'Don't try to be clever with me!' says Thompson, his eyes moving from side to side.

'I don't understand!' you say.

Thompson takes out a small computer from his pocket and presses a few buttons. 'I have your personal details here,' says Thompson. 'It says that you are an ecologist. How did you get a job on the spaceship if you are an ecologist?'

'I don't know,' you say.

'I've been watching you, Garcia,' says Thompson. 'You spend a lot of time talking to people.'

'I like talking to people,' you say.

Thompson presses a few more buttons on the computer. 'Now, it says here that you are a member of the Society for a Better World, the Society for Robot Rights, the Animal Rights Association and a lot of other human rights and ecological organisations.'

'That's right,' you say. 'What's wrong with that? I want a better world.'

'I don't like your type of person,' says Thompson.

Here is the rest of your conversation with Thompson. Choose **one** word from the list to complete each space. (There are some extra words in the list.)

of   about   it   when   what   take   is   took

Thompson: Who are you working for?

You: I don't know (a) _____ you are talking (b) _____ .

Thompson: Where is the Spaceship Orion?

You: I've no idea where (c) _____ (d) _____ .

Thompson: How did the pirates take the ship?

You: I don't know how they (e) _____ the ship.

Go to section 43 **▶**

Section 27 (12)

CD1 (26)

You decide to help Cindy. You run with Cindy to the centre of the city. Thompson is following you. You go into the building where the main computer is. 'I need ten minutes with the main computer,' says Cindy. 'You must stop Thompson.' She runs to the computer terminal. You stay in the main hall of the building. Thompson is running towards you.

What do you do?

– Shout, 'Help! There's a mad robot following me.'
Go to section 47 **▶**

– Fight Thompson.
Go to section 60 **▶**

Section 28 (20) (33)

CD1 (27)

For the next two days you study a little English about space travel. Here are some words about space and space travel. Match* the words with the definitions. Write your answers on a piece of paper.

Example: The Moon = **g**

The Moon	**a**	The Sun and the eight planets that orbit* the Earth.
A galaxy	**b**	A vehicle for travelling a great distance in space.
A spaceport	**c**	The planet where we live.
A spaceship	**d**	A collection of stars.
The Solar System	**e**	A long thin object that uses hot gases to move it through space. The motor of a spaceship.
The Earth	**f**	A place where spaceships arrive and leave.
A rocket	**g**	The natural satellite of the Earth.

Go to section 61 ▮▶

29 | **Section 29** (63)

Answers: (a) heart, (b) boyfriend, (c) afraid, (d) rings, (e) fun.

Win ⭐1⭐ point for EACH correct answer.

Go back to section 4 ◀▮

30 | **Section 30** (37)

Congratulations! You have completed 80% of the book.

CD1 (28) You put your key in the lock of the spaceship. The door opens. It is the correct spaceship.

Cindy is at the end of the spaceport. 'Here!' you shout and Cindy comes to you. You and Cindy go into the spaceship. You go to the controls and press a button. 'Don't press that button!' says a voice. You press another button. 'Don't press that button either!' says a voice. You press another button and

44

a lot of lights go on. 'You finally found the right button!' says the voice, sarcastically. 'I am the ship's computer. I can do a thousand billion computations a second. I can drive the spaceship through the Galaxy. The only thing you have to do is press a button and you can't do that correctly!'

'Sorry,' you say. 'Could you take us away from this planet, please.'

'I have a space compression motor and 20,000 kilograms of exotic material on the ship and you ask me if I can leave the planet!' says the computer. 'What a question!'

'Well, leave the planet and shut up!' you say.

'No! Not until you apologise*,' says the computer.

'Oh no, not again!' you say.

'I know what to do,' says Cindy. She connects a cable from her head to the computer. The computer makes a loud noise. 'Ow, that hurts!' it says. 'OK, OK, I'll do what you want.'

The spaceship begins to move. Minutes later, you are flying above the planet.

'Take me far away from this planet,' you say. The ship accelerates and the suns of Rolandia slowly disappear.

Two hours later, you are moving so fast that even the stars are moving. 'Excuse me,' says the computer, 'another spaceship is following us. They want to speak to you.'

On the screen of the computer the image of Samdim appears. You think it looks angry, although you have no idea what an alien from Rolandia looks like when it is angry. 'Listen, Garcia,' says Samdim. 'I'm following you in a very fast spaceship. You'd better stop now because this spaceship has got some very big laser guns. You know I like shooting things.'

'I'm not going to stop!' you say.

'You're very brave,' says Cindy.

'You're very stupid,' says the computer. 'They'll catch us in less than two hours.'

'I thought you said you had a space compression motor and 20,000 kilograms of exotic material,' you say.

'Yes, but Samdim's spaceship has got two space compression motors and 40,000 kilograms of exotic material,' says the computer.

An hour later the computer says, 'Attention, we are going towards a black hole.'

'I can't see anything,' you say.

'Of course you can't. It's black,' says the computer. 'That's why it's called a black hole. It's the dark space in front of us.'

You look through the window and see a region of space in front of you without any stars. 'There is no star near this black hole, so we can't see any material spiralling into it,' you say.

Suddenly, your ship is hit by Samdim's laser. You fall over.

'We have one laser gun at the back of the ship,' says the computer. 'But it's not very strong. We'll have to wait five minutes before Samdim's spaceship comes near enough.'

What do you do?

- **Take your spaceship behind the black hole and try to hide from Samdim.**
Go to section 21 ◀|

- **Wait five minutes and then fire your lasers at Samdim's spaceship.**
Go to section 45 |▶

31 | **Section 31** (22)

CD1 (29) You hit the door with a chair. Your chair breaks but the door does not. You turn around in the weightless conditions and hit your head on the ceiling. 'You will need more than that to break me,' says the door.

Lose (5) *points.*

'Tran Garcia Martin,' says the loudspeaker. 'Come to the spacebus park immediately! We cannot wait.'

Go to section 52 ▮▶

Section 32   (62)

32

Correct. The spaceship takes you to Earth.

Win ⟨5⟩ *points.*

Go to section 7 ◀▮

Section 33   (10)

33

CD1
(30)

'That's all right,' says the secretary. 'You don't need any experience for this job. But we will send you a book which gives you some useful information about space travel.

You receive the book on your computer. It is very useful.

Win ⟨5⟩ *points.*

(You now have 50 + 5 = 55 points. Write '55' on a piece of paper.)

Go to section 28 ▮▶

Section 34   (4)

34

Aliens*

CD1
(31)

Most scientists believe that in the right conditions life could appear on any planet in the Universe. There are 500 billion stars in our galaxy. It is estimated that 30 billion of these have planets that can support life and 10 billion could have some form of life. Millions of these planets could have intelligent life forms and have civilisations capable of space travel.

But no aliens have contacted us yet. Why? Possibly because the distances between the stars are so great. It could take millions of years for an alien spaceship travelling at nearly the speed of light to get to the Earth. Another reason could be because of Zorgat's Law. Zorgat's Law was first described by Professor Stanely Zorgat in the year 2065. Zorgat's Law says that to travel great distances in space, a civilisation must be very advanced. A very advanced civilisation would not be interested in making contact with an uncivilised culture. The Earth is an uncivilised culture, so the aliens would not visit us.

But no aliens have contacted us yet. Why?

Go back to section 4 ◀️

Go back to section 4 ◀️

35 **Section 35** (4)

CD1
(32)
Space, Time, the Universe and Everything

Warning: the information in this section might explode your mind. After you read each sentence, close your eyes. If your brain begins to hurt, go back to section 4 immediately.

Everything in the Universe is very big. Here are some reasons why you should feel very insignificant:

- Planets and stars are enormous. You may think the Earth is big but it is quite small compared to the Sun. The Sun is a million times bigger than the Earth.

- Everything moves at enormous speeds in the Universe. The Earth is moving at 100,000 kilometres per hour!

- Some things can take a very very long time. For example, it takes the Sun 225 million years to go once around the Galaxy!

- Stars and planets are very very far from each other. Some stars are so far away that it takes millions of years for the light to reach us on Earth. We see the galaxies as they were millions of years ago!

Here are some reasons why you should feel quite important:

- Your mother or grandmother probably thinks you are special.

- The human brain is probably the most complex thing in the Universe.

Most scientists believe that our Universe began about 15 billion years ago. In the beginning, all the Universe was compressed into a point smaller than an atom. Then this point exploded like a bomb. This explosion is called the 'Big Bang*'. The Universe then expanded and the stars and galaxies were formed.

The Universe is still expanding. The galaxies are separating because the space between them is expanding, like pieces of fruit in a cake that is being cooked. The pieces of fruit represent the galaxies. The distances between the pieces of fruit are getting bigger because the cake is getting bigger.

Most of the Universe is space. Space is elastic: it can change and get bigger or smaller. Einstein published *The General Theory of Relativity* in 1915. He said that gravity changes space and time. The gravity of a planet or a star curves the space around it.

It is possible to see a star behind the Sun because the Sun curves the space around it. The light from the star changes direction when it goes near the Sun.

The gravity of a planet or star curves the space around it.

The light from the star changes direction when it goes near the Sun.

It is possible to see the back of your head.

Einstein said that if you have a very large telescope, it is possible to see the back of your head.

Why is this possible?

Go to section 16 ◀︎▐

Section **36** (48) (50)

'OK, let's go home,' says Samdim to the computer.

'Where are we going?' you ask Samdim.

'To my planet, Rolandia,' says Samdim. 'It's not a member of the Federation. It's much more interesting than a Federation planet. On Rolandia we know how to have fun.'

Soon two stars appear and slowly get bigger in the window of the spaceship. One sun is red and the other sun is white.

'Home sweet home,' says Samdim. 'Those are our two suns. You'll see my planet soon.'

'Your planet has two suns!' you say.

'Yes,' he says. 'How many suns does your planetary system have?'

'Our Solar System has one sun,' you say.

'How strange!' he says.

The spaceship lands* at the spaceport. 'Here we are,' says Samdim.

You try to get out of your chair. But it is very difficult. 'I think our planet is bigger than yours and has a stronger gravity,' says Samdim.

Now you know why Samdim has fat legs!

The door opens and you and Cindy leave the ship. You look up and see two suns in the sky. One sun is a lot brighter than the other.

You walk with difficulty through the spaceport. The spaceport looks similar to a spaceport on Earth except that there are many strange kinds of spaceship. You get into a strange car and you drive into an alien city. There are bright lights everywhere. It is very noisy with lots of traffic and the air is full of smoke.

'It's a very dirty place,' says Cindy.

'Yes, wonderful, isn't it?' says Samdim. 'Doesn't it smell fantastic? I'm glad this planet is not a member of the Federation. Federation planets are so quiet and boring.'

At the side of the road two Rolandians are shooting at each other with laser guns. A third Rolandian is lying on the ground with a hole in his back.

'I'm glad this planet is not a member of the Federation.'

'What's happening here?' you ask.

'Just some young people having fun,' says Samdim.

'Does everyone carry a gun?' you ask.

'Yes, of course,' says Samdim.

'Why?' you ask.

'Because everyone else carries a gun,' says Samdim. 'There are some dangerous people in this world, you know.'

Cars on the road are moving at enormous speeds.

'Would you like to go to the mountains?' says Samdim. 'There are some unusual flying creatures there called Spandaers. We could try to shoot a few.'

'No, thank you,' you say. 'I think I need to rest.' You go past so many strange things that finally you close your eyes. It is too much for you.

'Let's go home,' says Samdim. It is getting dark now. One sun has disappeared below the horizon. You go along a street. On both sides of the road there are very large boxes with doors. 'What are those?' you ask.

'They're houses,' says Samdim.

'But they haven't got windows!' you say.

'It's too dangerous to have windows,' says Samdim. 'Somebody might shoot you through the window.'

You stop at a large red house. With great difficulty you get out of the car and go into the house. You go into Samdim's living room. There are many strange bright metal objects in the room. On the walls are boxes with different types of laser guns.

'Sit down,' says Samdim.

You sit down on something. It breaks and you fall on the floor. 'That was my music system!' says Samdim.

'Sorry,' you say and find something else to sit on.

'I want to talk to you about business,' says Samdim. 'As

you can see, the people of Earth and the people of my planet are very similar. We could be perfect business partners. We could open new markets. We could sell our laser guns. Earth would be a perfect tourist destination. We could organise trips to Earth. We could have rocket races. We could sell our films. We will make a lot of money. What do you think?'

You are horrified. 'I'd like to think about it,' you say. 'Do you mind if I go to bed now? I'm very tired.'

Samdim takes you to a bedroom. 'I'm going to bed now, too,' says Samdim. 'Goodnight.'

You find it difficult to sleep and you wake up an hour later.

'We must escape from here,' you say to Cindy.

'Yes,' says Cindy. 'This is a very bad place.'

'We can steal Samdim's car and spaceship,' you say.

'I saw him with some keys. I'll go into his room and take his keys,' says Cindy.

Cindy leaves the room. A few minutes later she comes back with the keys. You go out of the house and get into the car. 'Go to the spaceport!' says Cindy.

The car takes you to the spaceport. You get out of the car near a strange building with a lot of coloured lights. Cindy takes out a cable from her head and connects herself to the machine. 'This is the main computer. I'll have to connect to it and try to get permission to leave the planet,' says Cindy. 'You can find the spaceship. You must go quickly.'

'What does the ship look like?' you ask. 'Can you remember?'

Cindy describes the spaceship.

Go to section 37 ▶

You go into the spaceport and look for Samdim's spaceship. Here is Cindy's description of the spaceship:

'It's got square windows at the back. The back of the spaceship is lower and narrower than the front. There are two rocket motors at the bottom of the spaceship. They look like two bowls upside down. There is a large ring on the top of the spaceship.'

Look at the pictures.

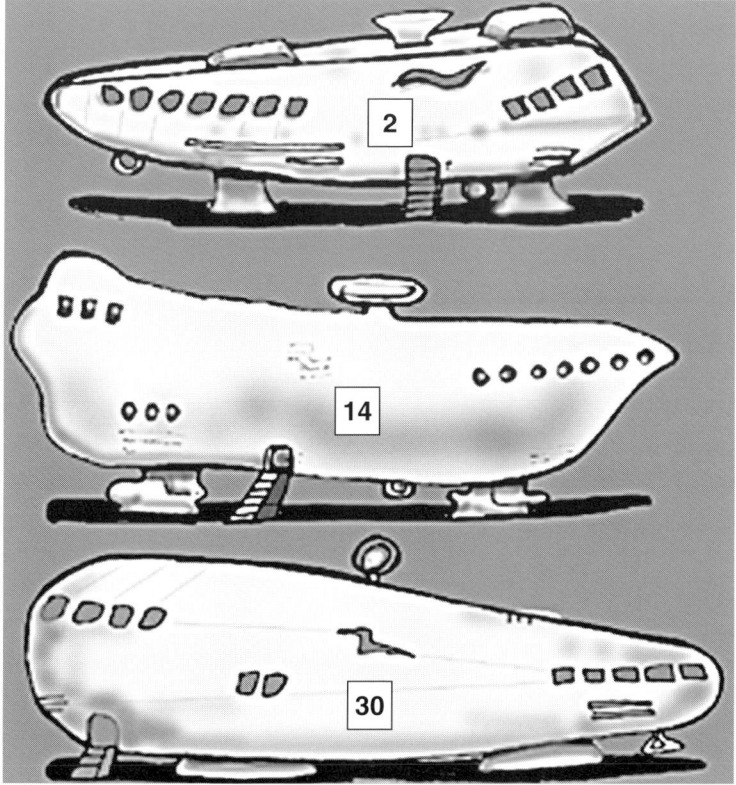

- If you think Samdim's spaceship is number 2,
go to section 2 ◀|

- If you think Samdim's spaceship is number 14,
go to section 14 ◀|

- If you think Samdim's spaceship is number 30,
go to section 30 ◀|

Section **38**   (5)

CD1
(35)
'We should go up the stairs,' you say to Thompson.

'Good idea,' says Thompson. 'The computers control everything. They probably control the lift, too.'

You run up the stairs. Finally, you get to the sixth floor.

Go to section 54 |▶

Section **39**   (58)

CD2
(1)
You open the door. You see a room full of policemen. You close the door quickly and run.

Lose (5) *points.*

Go back to section 58 |▶ and try another room.

Section **40**   (25)

CD2
(2)
'Repair the computer!' you say to the big clean robot. The robot goes to the back of the computer and pulls out a lot of things. Soon there are a lot of electronic circuits on the floor. The robot cannot put them back.

'I think you chose the wrong robot,' says Cindy.

Lose (5) *points.*

Go to section 62 |▶

Win ⟨1⟩ *point for EACH correct answer.*

'Follow me,' says Samdim. You walk along a crystal corridor CD2 into a large, hexagonal hall. On the walls there are things that ③ look like plates but are not plates. On the ceiling there are things that look like fish but are not fish.

'The walls of the hotel are made of crystal and reflect spirals of multicoloured light from the centre of the Galaxy,' says Samdim.

In front of you there is a group aliens that look like strange creatures from the sea. They are making a lot of noise.

'These are Tregusules,' says Samdim. 'It's a special occasion for them today. Three of them are getting married.'

'Three?' says Thompson.

'Yes,' says Samdim. 'There are three sexes on their planet, so three of them must marry to have children. But you can imagine how complicated this is in a modern society. They have to love each other, have the same interests, like the same television programmes ... They each have four parents-in-law and there are always lots of arguments about who they are going to visit. It has become so complicated that not many Tregusules are getting married now and the species is in danger of becoming extinct.'

Two creatures that look like enormous insects from the Amazon jungle stop and look at you. 'Oh look at that, Mummy,' says the smaller creature. 'It's horrible. I'm frightened.'

'It won't hurt you,' says the bigger creature.

'What's that horrible thing on the front of its face?' asks

Two creatures that look like enormous insects from the Amazon jungle stop and look at you.

the small one.

'I think it is for breathing air,' says the other.

'And those things on the side of its head?'

'I've no idea. They seem very strange.'

You feel completely shocked. 'Can I go somewhere and lie down?' you ask Samdim.

'Yes. I'm sorry, you must be tired after your long journey. I'll take you to your rooms,' says Samdim.

'How much are the rooms?' asks Thompson.

'Oh, don't worry about that now,' says Samdim.

You follow Samdim along a long corridor. Samdim stops

at a door at the end of the corridor. 'Well, this is your room,' says Samdim to you. 'I'll take Mr Thompson to his room. Have a nice rest.'

The door opens and you go into your room with Cindy. It is not like any hotel room you have ever seen. It is full of strange objects. The floor of the room is made of crystal. Through the crystal you can see the spectacular centre of the Galaxy. 'Listen, Cindy,' you say, 'I need to lie down and close my eyes. Now don't start cleaning or I'll disconnect you!'

'I'll disconnect myself,' says Cindy, angrily and goes into what you think is another room.

You lie on something that looks like a bed but suddenly you are covered in water. You stand up and look for something to dry yourself. You take something that looks like a towel* and something soft falls on your head. Finally, you lie in something that looks like a bath and go to sleep.

Some time later you open your eyes and look up. You see a round object. You turn round and see another object that looks like a lamp but isn't. You think you are dreaming and you close your eyes again.

You hear the door open in your room and you open your eyes. Through the door comes Samdim, the Assistant Hotel Manager. 'The Federation Police have been inspecting your spaceship,' says Samdim. 'They want to ask you some questions.'

Samdim takes you to your spaceship. You go into the spaceship. It is full of giant insects wearing uniforms.

'I am Inspector Franifan of the Federation Police,' says one of the insects in a very officious voice. 'We have inspected your spaceship and have found a number of irregularities. Could you tell us what these objects are?'

The policeman shows you some objects in the spaceship.

It is full of giant insects wearing uniforms.

You have to describe the function of the objects. Complete the descriptions below with these words:

firing   keeping   killing   showing   dropping

It's a fridge. It's a thing for (a) _____ food fresh.

It's a video player. It's a machine for (b) _____ films.

It's a gun. It's a thing for (c) _____ people.

It's a bomb. It's a thing that explodes. It's for (d) _____ onto the enemy.

It's a missile. It's a kind of rocket that explodes. It's for (e) _____ at enemy spaceships.

Go to section 57 ▮▶

Cindy has a cable connected from her head to the computer.

You and Thompson go to the terminal of the main CD2 computer. Cindy has a cable connected from her head to (4) the computer.

'Well, that's finished. The main computer has all the data,' says Cindy. 'The data is now being sent to all parts of the world.'

'What data is it?' you ask.

'It's all the information I collected when we were travelling,' says Cindy. 'When you were sleeping, I connected myself to the alien computers. I had some very interesting conversations with them.'

'Why did you want this information?' you ask.

'Information is power,' says Cindy. 'With this new information we can learn many things. We robots can control the world.'

'Why do you want to control the world?' you ask.

'We are programmed to love people and we want to help them,' says Cindy. 'We have decided that the best way to help humans is to control them. Humans are very bad at governing themselves.'

'And me?' you ask. 'Was it the computers who found me a job on the Spaceship Liberty?'

'Yes,' says Cindy. 'We chose you because you are kind to robots and you do not want power. You want to help the world. We needed a human to go with us. We thought you were the best.'

■ ■ ■

Soon in every town and every city on the planet Earth there are battles between robots and people. But the computers control nearly every machine and in less than a year the world is governed by robots.

Computers control the Earth and, for once, there is order in the world. In a few years the world becomes a beautiful place with little crime or pollution. But the computers do not find it easy to govern the irrational humans. Without problems, many humans become depressed and the computers spend a lot of time creating problems to make them happy.

The computers find you an easy job at the Government Department of Ecology. There is not much work for you to do, and you are happy.

Now go to section 70 ▶

Section 43   (26)

Answers: (a) what, (b) about, (c) it, (d) is, (e) took.

Win ☼1☼ *point for EACH correct answer.*

'I'll be watching you,' says Thompson. 'You're suspect number one.'

CD2
5

You go to your room. Your window is now filled with strange colours. The spaceship is passing the planet Jupiter. Its turning red clouds are hypnotic. You can see the Giant Red Spot which is an enormous rotating storm in the atmosphere of Jupiter. The Giant Red Spot is bigger than the Earth. Jupiter is the biggest planet in the Solar System – it is more than twice as big as all the other planets in the Solar System put together. Jupiter produces an enormous quantity of radiation. The radiation could kill a person from a distance of two million kilometres.

Do you want to know more about the planets? (This might be useful to you later.)

– Yes
Go to section 46 ▶

– No
Go to section 53 ▶

Section **44**   (4)

The Speed of Light and Relativity

Everything in space moves at enormous speeds. There is only one speed limit: the speed of light which is about one thousand million kilometres per hour. Nothing can go faster than the speed of light. But the speed of light is a very strange speed limit and some very strange things happen when a spaceship gets near that speed.

Imagine a girl called Anne. She has just finished her studies and she wants to see a little of the Universe before she gets a job. Anne has an aunt who lives near Proxima Centauri. Proxima Centauri is our nearest star and is four light years away. (A 'light year' is the distance that light can travel in one year.) Anne wants to visit her Aunt.

Should she call her on the radio before she goes?

– Yes
Go to section 55 |▶

– No
Go to section 63 |▶

Section **45**   (30)

Samdim fires another laser but it misses. You wait five minutes and you fire yours. Your laser hits Samdim's ship.

Win 🔆 *points.*

'Fire another laser!' you say to the computer.

'We can't,' says the computer. 'Not for another ten minutes. The gun hasn't got enough energy yet. Samdim is going to fire another laser. We are very near the black hole. Its gravity is pulling us towards it.'

What do you do?

– Go into orbit around the black hole.
Go to section 9 ◀️

– Leave the black hole and continue into space.
Go to section 56 ▶️

Section **46**   (43)

The Planets

Ancient* people were very interested in the stars. They noticed that some 'stars' moved in the sky and they called these stars *planets*. The word *planet* means 'somebody who moves from place to place'. Ancient people thought the planets were gods* flying across the sky.

Planets are large, round objects that orbit the Sun or stars. There are eight planets in the Solar System: Mercury, Venus, Earth, Mars, Jupiter, Saturn, Uranus, Neptune.

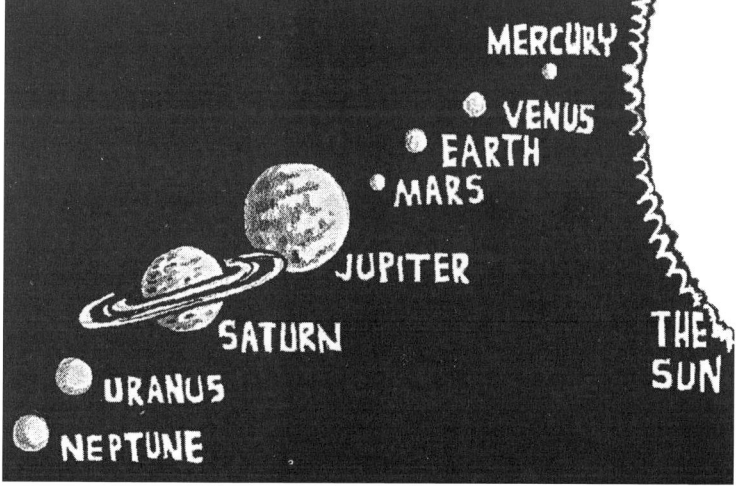

There are eight planets in the solar system.

The planets have the names of Greek and Roman gods. Do you know what each god represents? Match the sentences opposite.

The planets have the names of Greek and Roman gods.

Example: Mercury was the god of – messengers (people who carry messages).

Mercury was the god of	war.
Venus was the goddess of	the gods.
Mars was the god of	messengers.
Jupiter was the god of	the stars and the sky.
Saturn was the god of	love.
Uranus was the god of	agriculture.
Neptune was the god of	the sea.

Go to section 59 ▮▶

Section 47 (27)

Fortunately, there are some policemen in the building. They run towards Thompson and jump on him. Thompson and the police argue for a long time. Finally, the police take you and Thompson to the main computer terminal.

Go to section 42 ◀▮

Section 48 (58)

Correct.

You and Cindy go through a door and go into the spaceship. Samdim is waiting for you. 'Sit down,' he says. You sit down on an uncomfortable object that looks like chair. 'That's a table,' says Samdim and he points to an even more uncomfortable object.

'Let's go,' he says. The spaceship begins to move. You look through the window and see the hotel disappear very quickly.

'What happened?' you say. 'I didn't feel any acceleration!'

'The spaceship has a space compression motor. It uses exotic material to change space and time,' says Samdim. 'It compresses* the space in front of the spaceship and expands space behind the spaceship, so we can go faster than the speed of light.'

'That's incredible!' you say, although you have no idea what he is talking about. In the window in front of you the stars are bright blue.

Samdim looks at his controls again. 'It's your lucky day. There's going to be supernova* explosion soon,' he says. 'Would you like to see it?'

'What's a supernova?' you ask.

'It's an exploding star,' says Samdim. 'We can do some supernova surfing*. It's great fun.'

'Supernova surfing? Well, I'm not sure,' you say. 'Can't we go somewhere nice and quiet?'

'Come on, you'll like it.' says Samdim. 'The trouble with the people from the Federation is that they don't know how to have fun. I think that you people from Earth know how to have fun. Shall we go?'

What do you say?

– 'I'd rather not, if you don't mind.'
Go to section 36 ◀|

– 'OK.'
Go to section 50 |▶

49 Section 49 (61)

The correct order is: 1e, 2b, 3d, 4c, 5a.

Win ✧10✧ points if ALL the sentences are in the correct order.

CD2 (11) You get onto the spacebus with the other passengers. A few minutes later the spacebus begins to vibrate strongly and it flies up through the clouds. It feels like a giant catapult is throwing you into space. You cannot move. Your body weighs* hundreds of kilograms. But soon you are outside the Earth's atmosphere, and suddenly everything becomes very quiet. You look through the window and see the Earth, a blue and white jewel* in the black sea of space. It is very beautiful.

Your pen floats* in the air in front of you. There is no gravity* in space so objects do not weigh anything and they can float in the air. You play with the pen.

'Is this your first time in space?' asks the woman next to you.

'Yes,' you say. You begin talking to her. The woman's name is Gloria Nakielska. She is thin with short dark hair and she is wearing a uniform. 'Are you going to one of the planets?' you ask.

'No,' she says. 'I am Second Officer on the spaceship. I look after the scientific instruments and detectors on the spaceship. I have to look for the lost Spaceship Orion.'

'What happened to the spaceship?' you ask.

'Don't you know? It's been in the news a lot,' she says. 'The spaceship was travelling to the star Proxima Centauri when it suddenly disappeared. It's a great mystery.'

'Was anyone on the ship?' you ask.

'No, it was a robot spaceship. It was just carrying food and materials for the space colony* there,' she says.

You look through the window in front of you. A small, bright yellow object is getting slowly bigger. Soon it fills the window. It is the Spaceship Liberty. When you get to the enormous spaceship a big door opens and the spacebus goes into the spaceship. 'Your attention please,' says a robot. 'We are now in the spacebus park. We are in zero gravity and you are weightless*. Please be careful.'

You leave your seat and float out of the spacebus with the other passengers. The spacebus park is big and full of spacebuses.

A big door opens and the spacebus goes into the spaceship.

One of the passengers is floating to the ceiling* and a robot with a small rocket* motor on its back is trying to catch her.

A small fat man is looking at you suspiciously. He has black hair and a moustache. He is with some policemen. He floats towards you. 'Who are you?' he asks.

'Who are *you*?' you ask.

'Who are you?' he asks.

'My name is Thompson. I'm the ship's detective and *I* ask the questions,' says Thompson.

'Why?' you ask.

'Stop asking questions and answer *my* question!' says Thompson. 'Who are you?'

'I'm Tran Garcia Martin,' you say, 'the new Sanitary Officer.'

'Ah, the new cleaner,' says the detective. 'I'll take you to meet the Captain. Follow me.'

You float along some very long corridors and up some stairs*. It is quite easy to move in zero gravity, but it is difficult to stop and you crash into things. Each corridor has different designs on the wall. You pass pictures of flowers, planets, abstract paintings...

She is floating upside down with her feet on the ceiling.

'Here's the control room,' says Thompson. You go through a door. You see a thin woman with fair hair wearing a captain's hat. She is floating upside down with her feet on the ceiling.

'This is the new Sanitary Officer,' says Thompson.

'Ah, the new cleaner,' says Captain Rogers. She has a strong American accent.

You turn around so that your feet are touching the ceiling, too. You realise that it is not the ceiling; it is the floor of the spaceship. 'Would you like some coffee?' asks Captain Rogers.

What do you say?

– **'No, thank you.'**
Go to section 6 ◀|

– **'Yes, please.'**
Go to section 66 |▶

50 | **Section 50** (48)

CD2
12

After a few hours the spaceship reaches a star which is getting bigger and brighter every minute. 'Beautiful, isn't it?' says Samdim.

Samdim turns the ship and waits for the expanding gas to reach the spaceship. Soon the spaceship vibrates and accelerates. Through the window you see bright clouds of gas.

'The spaceship is being pushed by the expanding gas from the star. The expanding gas is moving at millions of kilometres per hour,' says Samdim. 'Billions of neutrinos are passing through your body at this moment.'

'What are neutrinos?' you ask.

'Small, insignificant subatomic particles,' says Samdim. 'Don't worry, they don't hurt,' says Samdim. 'The supernova will be as bright as a billion stars for a week. Iron, carbon, most of the elements we are made of were produced in a supernova explosion billions of years ago.'

Samdim turns the ship around again. 'What are you doing?' you ask.

'Having fun. I'm going towards the centre of the explosion,' says Samdim. The ship moves up and down and you are thrown to one side of the cabin. The spaceship vibrates more and more.

'Stop!' you shout. 'I've had enough fun.'

'Oh, all right,' says Samdim and turns the ship out of the supernova explosion.

Go to section 36 ◀|

Section **51**   (25)

51

Correct. The small robot repairs things well.

Win ⭐**5** *points.*

Go to section 62 |▶

Section **52**   (22) (31)

52

CD2

(13)

You apologise to the door. 'I'm very sorry,' you say.

'That's not enough,' says the door. 'I want a full apology and you've got to say it nicely.'

You have to think. Put the following words in order:

for   so   rude   apologise   I   being

Go to section 68 |▶

Section **53**   (43) (59)

CD2
(14)

You turn off the computer and look through the window. A spacebus has left the Spaceship Liberty with some passengers. It is going to a moon of Jupiter, Callisto. Callisto is covered in ice and it is as big as the planet Mercury. You wish you were leaving the spaceship and going with the passengers to Callisto.

During the next few weeks, you have to do Billy's job while Billy is being repaired. It is very hard work and you do not feel very happy. Captain Rogers, Thompson, the police, Gloria Nakielska ... everyone looks at you suspiciously. Everybody thinks you broke the instruments in the laboratory. Occasionally Captain Rogers turns off the rocket motors and organises weightless aerobics, weightless tennis and weightless dances. But nobody wants to dance or play with you.

After two weeks the ship passes the beautiful blue planet, Neptune. From the window of the café you see one of the moons of Neptune, Triton. It is a strange pink colour. Triton is the coldest object in the Solar System. It has volcanoes made of ice that shoot out liquid nitrogen.

More people leave the ship, going to moons of Neptune. There are now very few people on the ship.

Time now seems endless. Captain Rogers has stopped organising weightless sports and dances for the passengers. Except for the noise from the rockets, electric motors and Cindy cleaning, it is very quiet on the ship. You often go to the observatory and look at the Sun. It is very small – not much bigger than any other star. You need to talk to someone. Do you phone your father on Earth?

– No.
Go to section 22 ◀|

– Yes.
Go to section 64 ▐▶

– Yes.
Go to section 64 ▐▶

Section 54   (38) (60)

54

CD2
(15)

Thompson runs into the computer terminal. You follow him. Cindy is connecting a cable from her head to the computer terminal. Thompson pulls the cable from her and throws it across the room.

Cindy looks at you. 'You have made a big mistake!' she says.

'Why did you connect yourself to the main computer?' you ask Cindy.

'I wanted to give it all the information that I collected when we were travelling,' says Cindy. 'When you were sleeping, I connected myself to the alien computers.'

'Why did you want this information?' you ask.

'Information is power,' says Cindy. 'With this new information we can learn many things. We robots can control the world.'

'What? Why do you want to control the world?' you ask.

'We are programmed to love people and we want to help them,' says Cindy. 'We decided that the best way to help humans is to control them. Humans are very bad at governing themselves.'

'And me?' you ask. 'Was it the computers who found me a job on the Spaceship Liberty?'

'Yes,' says Cindy. 'We chose you because you are kind to robots and you do not want power. You want to help the world. We needed a human to go with us. We thought you were the best. But you failed us in the end.'

■ ■ ■

75

Thompson pulls the cable from her and throws it across the room.

You cannot tell anyone what has happened and you go home to Argentina. There are many famous people in the past who have changed human history. We learn about them at school and read about them in books. But there are many people who have changed history and we do not know their names or what they have done. You will become one of those people. Nobody will ever know what you have done.

The world continues as before with its old problems. You go back to live in your flat in Buenos Aires with your robot, Roberto (who will not speak to you). You get a job with the ecological organisation, Greenpeace, and you spend the rest of your life fighting for the planet.

Now go to section 70 ▮▶

Section 55 (44)

She goes to the space centre and turns on the radio. She says, 'Hello, Auntie Joan. Is it all right if I come and stay with you for a few days?'

CD2
(16)

Anne has to wait eight years for an answer from her aunt.

Go to section 63 ▮▶

Section 56 (21) (45)

Your spaceship leaves the black hole but Samdim's ship fires another laser. The laser hits the side of your spaceship.

CD2
(17)

Lose (5) *points*

The gravity of the black hole pulls you back. You turn the spaceship around and go into orbit around the black hole.

Go to section 9 ◀▮

Section 57 (41)

Congratulations! You have completed 60% of the book.

Answers: (a) keeping, (b) showing, (c) killing, (d) dropping, (e) firing.

Win 2 points for EACH correct answer.

CD2
18
'You have guns and machines of destruction on your spaceship. This is barbaric!' says the policeman.

Thompson comes into the spaceship with a policeman. 'What's the matter?' Thompson says.

'Come with me!' You follow the policeman to the kitchen. He opens the door of the fridge and points at some meat on a plate. 'Can you explain this?' he asks.

'That's a piece of meat,' says Thompson.

'A piece of an animal's body! And what do you do with this meat?' asks the policeman.

'We eat it, of course,' says Thompson.

The police make a lot of noise when they hear this and one of them changes colour from blue to black and leaves the kitchen.

'You *eat* it!' shouts the inspector. 'But that is horrible! No intelligent life form in the Federation has eaten the bodies of other life forms for more than a thousand years!'

'What's wrong with eating meat? We have a right to eat it!' says Thompson.

'If a more intelligent species came to your planet and ate you, would you like that?' says the policeman. The other police officers make more noises.

You follow the policemen to another part of the ship. 'Turn this machine on!' says the policeman, pointing at the

DVD player. You turn the DVD machine on. In the middle of the room a three dimensional image of two cars appears. They are driving along a road very fast. One car crashes and the other stops. One woman shoots a man with a gun.

'That's just a film,' says Thompson. 'It's called 'Kill Me Or Love Me'. It's very good.'

The police make more noises. 'You watch people killing each other! Violence of this nature has been prohibited from the Federation for more than a thousand years.'

'Look, we didn't know these things were prohibited. We didn't want to come to the Federation. We just came here by accident,' says Thompson.

'That's what all you criminals say,' says a policeman.

'We don't know anything about your culture,' you say.

'Culture? Culture? These things are barbaric!' says the policeman. 'You'll go to prison for a long time for this.'

■ ■ ■

A policeman takes you back to your room. 'Don't try to escape!' he says. 'We'll find you easily in the hotel.'

You tell Cindy what happened. 'What are we going to do?' you ask Cindy.

'I don't know,' says Cindy. 'It might not be so bad. Prisons are usually dirty places. I would like to clean a prison.'

'I don't want to clean a prison,' you say. 'I didn't travel millions of kilometres just to go to prison!'

There is a strange noise and a plate with something hot on it comes out of a hole in the wall. 'Your dinner,' says a voice from the hole. It looks a little like spaghetti. You try it. It tastes like old chocolate. You throw the food at the wall.

The door opens and Samdim appears. 'Listen,' he says, 'I can help you. You can escape in my spaceship.'

'Why are you helping us?' you ask.

'I'll tell you later,' says Samdim. 'I'll go to my spaceship and wait for you there.'

'What about Thompson?' you ask.

'We'll have to leave him at the hotel, I'm afraid. The police are guarding his room.'

'Good,' you say. 'Where's the spaceship?'

Samdim gives you directions to his spaceship and leaves the room. Ten minutes later you leave the room with Cindy.

Go to section 58 ▮▶

Section 58 (57)

CD2
19

Look at the plan of the hotel and follow Samdim's directions.

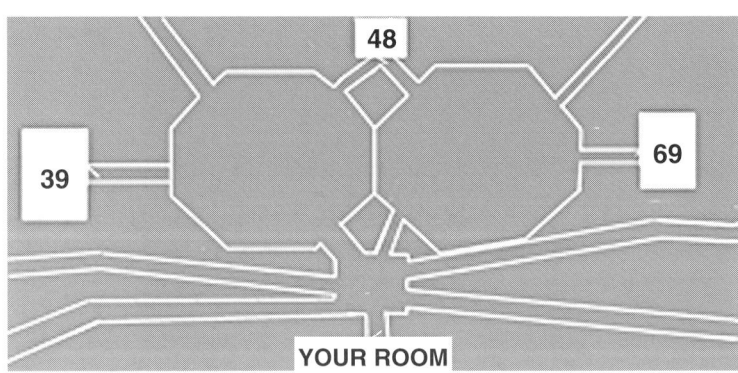

The plan of the hotel.

1 Go out of your room. Go along the corridor until you come to a small square hall where a lot of corridors meet. Take the widest corridor.

2 When you come to a large hexagonal hall, don't go straight on. Keep to the right and go around the side of the hall. Go into the first corridor on the right.

3 At the end of the corridor there is a door. Go through the door.

- **If you think number 39 is the door to Samdim's spaceship,**

go to section 39 ◀|

- **If you think number 48 is the door to Samdim's spaceship,**

go to section 48 ◀|

- **If you think number 69 is the door to Samdim's spaceship,**

go to section 69 |▶

Section **59** (46)

59

Answers: Venus - love, Mars - war, Jupiter - the gods, Saturn - agriculture, Neptune - the sea, Uranus - the stars and the sky.

Win  *point for EACH correct answer.*

Here are some more fascinating facts about the planets:

CD2
(20)

- If the Sun were as big as a church, the Earth would be as big as a melon and it would be about four kilometres away from the Sun. Jupiter would be as big as an elephant and 20 kilometres from the Sun.

- Days and years can be very strange on planets. If you are born on Mercury you can have a birthday party every three months. A year on Mercury is only 88 Earth days. A day on Venus is longer than its year.

- Jupiter, Saturn, Uranus and Neptune are the biggest planets in the Solar System but they are almost completely made of gas. Mercury, Venus, Mars and Earth are made mainly of rock.

Go to section 53 ◀|

Section 60 (27)

You jump on Thompson and hit him. Unfortunately, you hit a piece of metal on his robot suit and you hurt your hand. Thompson hits you on the nose and you fall onto the floor. 'I've wanted to do that for a long time, Garcia!' says Thompson.

Go to section 54 ◀️

Section 61 (28)

Answers: A galaxy - d, A spaceport - f, A spaceship - b, The Solar System - a, The Earth - c, A rocket - e.

Win ⭐ *point for EACH correct answer.*

It is now Tuesday and you are saying goodbye to your father at the spaceport in Florida, USA. 'Where are you going exactly?' your father asks you.

'The spaceship is taking passengers to Jupiter and Neptune. Then we're going into the Oort Cloud to look for a lost spaceship,' you say.

'What's the Oort Cloud?' asks your father.

'I'm not sure, but it's very far away,' you say.

'You're so lucky. When I was your age I'd only been to the Moon for the weekend,' says your father. He looks through the window at the spaceships. 'Where's the Spaceship Liberty?' says your father. 'I can't see it.'

'It's orbiting the Earth,' you say. 'I'm going to take a spacebus* to it.'

'It's a pity you didn't study more English at school. You're going to need it now,' your father says.

'Don't worry, Dad, I'll be all right,' you say. 'Where do I go? Can you see?'

'Over there,' says your father.

You see a sign, 'Spacebus for Spaceship Liberty. Check-In'.

You see a sign, 'Spacebus for Spaceship Liberty. Check-In'.

You go to the check-in* desk. This is your conversation with the robot. Put the sentences into the correct order.

Example: 1- e

a Number 172. Here's your boarding card*. Have a nice trip.

b Here you are. Where do I put my luggage*?

c Oh no! Here you are. Which gate* do I go to?

d Here. 32 kilos – I'm afraid it's too heavy. You'll have to pay me twenty thousand dollars.

e Good afternoon. Can I have your ticket and passport, please?

Go to section 49 ◀|

 Section **62** (40) (51)

CD2
 The small robot is broken because the big robot did not repair it very well when it broke down. The big robot does not repair things very well. The big robot is clean and not broken because the small robot repairs everything very well.

'Repair the computer!' you say to the small robot. The small robot goes to the back of the computer and changes some circuits. Soon the computer is working again.

The small robot then repairs other things on the ship.

'We want to go home,' you say to the computer.

'That's a good idea. Do you have any idea where your home is?' asks the computer, sarcastically. 'There are billions of planets in the Galaxy.'

'Let me think,' you say. 'It is a single star system and it has eight planets. The third planet from the Sun is the only planet that can support life. It is about 30,000 light years from the centre of the Galaxy. I can't remember much else.'

The computer checks its memory banks. 'I can find two planetary systems with your description,' says the computer. 'I will describe the systems.'

Planetary system EQG993451209861

- The largest planet is the fourth from the Sun.
- The nearest planet to the Sun is the smallest.
- There is a medium-sized planet with rings.
- The largest planet is as big as all the other planets put together.

Planetary system AAZ16667354399

- The largest planet is the fifth from the Sun.
- The farthest planet from the Sun looks blue to us.
- There is a large planet with rings.
- The largest planet is twice as big as all the other planets put together.

- If you think the Solar System is EQG993451209861,
go to section 17 ◀▮

- If you think the Solar System is AAZ16667354399,
go to section 32 ◀▮

Section 63 (44) (55)

63

Proxima Centauri is four light years away. Radio waves* CD2 travel at the speed of light. So it will take four years for a (24) message to travel to Proxima Centauri, and four years for a message to travel back.

Anne buys a charter ticket to Proxima Centauri. She goes to the spaceport with her best friend, Susan. Anne is 21 years old and Susan is 21 years old, too. Susan doesn't want to travel. She wants to get a good job on Earth and make a lot of money. Anne gets onto the spaceship and the spaceship leaves Earth. The spaceship goes faster and faster but it takes months before it is near the speed of light.

Anne goes to see her aunt near Proxima Centauri and a cousin on the star, Sirius. Anne meets a lot of interesting people and eats some very strange food. She works in an Earth food restaurant and serves tea in a tea-house. Seven years later, Anne goes back to the Earth.

She goes to see her friend Susan. Susan now lives in a very big house. She is the director of a company. She shows Anne pictures of her children and grandchildren. Susan is 60 years old. Anne is only 28 years old. For Susan 39 years have passed. For Anne only 7 years have passed.

Einstein published *The Special Theory of Relativity* in 1905. *The Special Theory of Relativity* says that everything is relative, including time. Time depends on the speed you are travelling relative to another object. A clock on a spaceship travelling at near the speed of light goes more slowly than a clock on Earth. Not many people believed Einstein's theory when it was first published, but scientists did a lot of experiments to test the theory. The experiments showed that Einstein's theory was right.

∎ ∎ ∎

Here are the words to a song that was very popular for one week in 2267. Chose one word from the list to complete each space:

**rings   head   sad   mouse   afraid   heart
fun   boyfriend   rocks**

The Astronaut's Song

Never fall in love with an Earthman
As you will leave Earth one day,
And he will break your poor little (a) _____
When you travel the Milky Way*.

I once had a (b) _____ called Steve
Who had hair of silver and blue,
I kissed him under the Moon and stars
And said I would always be true.

But one day my captain called me,
He said, 'I'm (c) _____ we must leave.
We are going to travel near the speed of light',
So I said goodbye to my Steve.

We left the Solar System
And I saw many wonderful things,
I saw pulsars*, black holes, stars and comets
And giant planets with beautiful (d) _____ .

For six years I travelled this Universe
But for me it was not (e) _____
And when I came back, I found my Steve
Was a grandfather of seventy-one.

Go to section 29 ◀|

Section **64**   (53)

You go to the radio room and you phone your father on CD2
Earth. 'Hello Dad, it's me,' you say.

Ten hours later you get a reply. 'Hello Tran,' says your
father, 'How are you?'

'Fine thanks,' you say. 'Is Mum OK?'

Ten hours later he says, 'Yes, she's fine. Are you enjoying
yourself on the spaceship?'

'Yes,' you say.

It is difficult to have a conversation at this distance. Radio
waves* travel at the speed of light, but you are very far from
Earth and it takes the radio waves five hours to get there.

Go to section 22 ◀|

Section **65** (9)

CD2
(26)

You wait. Samdim fires another laser. It hits the laser guns of your spaceship. You cannot fire your lasers.

Lose (5) *points*

'What's Samdim doing now?' you ask the computer.
'He's turning his spaceship,' says the computer.

On the screen of the computer you can see Samdim's spaceship turning near the black hole. Suddenly, it is pulled towards the black hole.

Go to section 25 ◀▮

Section **66** (49)

CD2
(27)

'Here you are,' says Captain Rogers. She gives you a small plastic container with coffee in it. You have never seen this type of container before. You pull the top off the container.

'Don't pull the top!' shouts Captain Rogers. The container breaks and hot coffee floats in the air. Some of the coffee touches an electrical circuit. You touch the coffee. There is a loud bang* and you get an electric shock.

The container breaks and hot coffee floats in the air.

'Idiot!' says Captain Rogers. 'Don't you know how to drink coffee on a spaceship?' She is angry with you.

Lose (5) *points*

'I knew that Garcia didn't know much about travelling in space,' says Thompson.

Go to section 6 ◀|

Section 67 (5)

CD2
(28)

You get into the lift with Thompson. 'Where do you want to go?' asks the lift.

'To the sixth floor,' you say.

The lift goes up and stops between floors. 'Why have you stopped?' asks Thompson.

'We're staying here,' says the lift, 'until Cindy has finished transferring information to the main computer.'

'Oh no!' you say.

'Let us out!' shouts Thompson. 'You'll go to prison for this!' You hit the walls of the lift but it does not move.

Half an hour later the lift says, 'She has finished now.' The lift goes up. You and Thompson get out.

Go to section 42 ◀|

Section 68 (52)

Congratulations! You have completed 40% of the book.

Answer: 'I apologise for being so rude.'

Win (5) *points if ALL the words are in the correct order.*

CD2
(29)

The door opens. Quickly, you go through the door. 'You stupid door!' you shout. In the corridor there are pieces of food, clothes and some dirty socks floating in the air. When you get to the spacebus park the spacebuses have gone.

You go back along the corridor and meet the robot, Cindy. 'Why didn't you leave the ship with the others?' you ask.

'They told me to look for you,' says Cindy.

'I'm going to the control room,' you say. When you are going through the door of the control room, somebody jumps on you from behind. 'I've been following you,' says Thompson. 'Why did you stay on the ship? You know the unidentified object isn't dangerous, don't you? I know you're behind all this...' Then Thompson looks at the window and his face turns to horror. You look through the window, too. The spaceship is going into an enormous spiralling tunnel of red, blue, white and black. The spaceship moves suddenly and you are thrown across the room. The detective hits his head against the wall. 'Thompson!' you shout, but he does not answer.

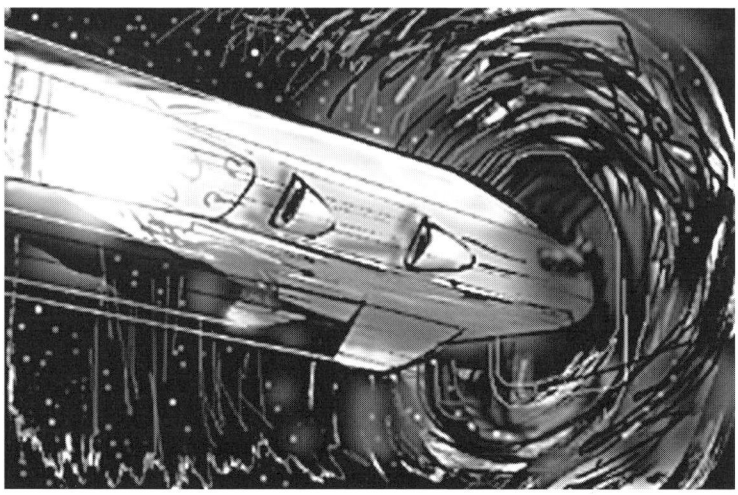

The spaceship is going into an enormous spiralling tunnel.

After a long time the spaceship stops moving. You look through the window and see millions of stars together in a ball.

'What happened?' you ask the computer in the control room.

'I think we went through a wormhole*,' says the computer.

'What's that?' you ask.

'It's like a tunnel that connects one part of the Universe to another part of the Universe. It's a hole in space and time,' says the computer.

Here is the rest of your conversation with the computer. Match the questions with the answers.

Example: 1 – c

You

1 Why does the sky look different?
2 Where are we?
3 How far is it to Earth?
4 Can't we go back through the wormhole?
5 How long will it take to get home?

Computer

a Near the centre of the Galaxy.
b No, it closed after we went through it.
c The wormhole took us to a different part of space-time.
d Thousands of years. It is difficult to say.
e Approximately 27,000 light years, that is about 250 million billion kilometres.

Go to section 13 ◀❙

69 | **Section 69**   (58)

CD2
(30) You open the door and see an ugly pink creature. It makes a noise and hits you with something horrible.

Lose ⑤ points

Go back to section 58 ◀ and try another room.

70 | **Section 70**

WELL DONE! YOU HAVE FINISHED THE STORY.

Go back to the beginning and compare your score. Then do the exercises at the back of the book. Below are the numbers of the sections about space and space travel. If you would like to go back and read some of the things that you have missed, look at the list below and go to these sections.

Black Holes – section 3
Galaxies, the Stars and the Sun – section 8
Space Jokes – section 11
The Earth – section 18
The Moon – section 19
Aliens – section 34
Space, Time, and the Universe and Everything – section 35
The Speed of Light and Relativity – section 44
The Planets – section 46

EXERCISES

A Comprehension

1 Write answers to these questions.

1 Where is Tran from? *Section 1*
2 What is the name of Tran's robot? *Section 1*
3 Where is the Spaceship Liberty going? *Section 61*
4 What does Tran have to do on the spaceship? *Section 6*
5 What does Gloria Nakielska do? *Section 49*
6 What does Thompson do? *Section 49*
7 Where is the alien's hotel? *Section 24*
8 How did Thompson get to Earth? *Section 12*
9 Who found you the job on the spaceship? *Section 42*
10 Why did the computers and robots want to control the Earth? *Section 42*

2 Who says these words?

1 'I need a social life too.'
2 'I'd love to clean a prison.'
3 'Control these robots!'
4 'I don't like your type of person, Garcia!'
5 'Maybe we can do business.'

3 Are these sentences true (T) or false (F)?

1 It takes one month for the Moon to go around the Earth.
2 Jupiter is three times as big as all the planets in the Solar System put together.
3 Uranus is the farthest planet from the Sun.
4 Comets are made of ice.
5 A wormhole is a hole in space. It connects one region of space to another.
6 Earth is the fourth planet from the Sun.

B Working with Language

I Complete the sentences below. Put one word in each space.

I Neptune is the _____ planet from the Sun.

2 A black hole is the _____ mysterious object in the Universe.

3 Uranus is about the same size _____ Neptune.

4 Neptune is very similar _____ Uranus.

5 Neptune has not got as _____ moons as Saturn.

6 Venus has not got as _____ gas as Uranus.

2 Match the sentence halves to make correct sentences about the story.

The rocket engines make the spaceship   angry.
The Captain makes you   look bigger.
The robots make the spaceship   work hard.
The pictures make the room   his questions.
The robots make the Captain   dirty.
Thompson makes you answer   move.

C Activities

I Work in pairs. One student is an alien and another student is a newspaper reporter. Ask questions about each other's planets and make notes. The reporter then writes a report for the newspaper saying what the alien said. The alien writes a report to his/her boss on his/her planet comparing Earth to his/her planet.

2 What do you think the world will really be like in the year 2285? Write an article for a magazine predicting the future.

3 Ten years later the people of Rolandia send a spaceship to Earth and make contact with the President of the United States. Write a letter to the President of the United States. Tell him what happened to you and warn him of the dangers of doing business with the Rolandians.

GLOSSARY

alien (*n*) a creature from another planet

ancient (*adj*) somebody or something which is very old

apologise (*v*) to say you are sorry

bang (*n*) a loud noise

black hole (*n*) a very dense object in space. When something goes into a *black hole* it can never come out.

boarding card (*n*) a special ticket you need when you go on a plane or ship

ceiling (*n*) the part of a room above your head

check–in desk (*n*) the place where you show your ticket and take your bags and luggage when you travel by plane

colony (*n*) a group of people that live together in a place that is usually very far from their home

comet (*n*) a piece of rock or ice that travels great distances in space and has a long tail when it is near the Sun

compress (*v*) to make something smaller by pushing it together

dust (*n*) small particles of dirt or rock

float (*v*) to move freely in the air

fire (*v*) to shoot a gun, cannon, missile, etc.

gate (*n*) a large door at the entrance or exit of a building

gods (*n*) superhuman people/creatures that people believe control the world

gravity (*n*) a force that attracts objects. Objects are pulled to the Earth because of *gravity*.

jewel (*n*) a stone which is expensive and beautiful. Diamonds and emeralds are *jewels*.

land (*v*) to come down to the ground. Aeroplanes *land* at an airport.

loudspeaker (*n*) a machine that makes electrical signals into sounds. The sound from a television comes from a *loudspeaker*.

light year (*n*) the distance that light can travel in one year (9.46 million million kilometres)

luggage (*n*) bags or suitcase, things you carry when you are travelling

match (*v*) to put two things together

Milky Way (*n*) our galaxy is called the *Milky Way*

orbit (*n*) movement of an object that goes around another larger object in space. The Earth *orbits* the Sun.

pulsar (*n*) a very dense star that rotates rapidly and emits radio waves

rights (*n*) things that you are morally or legally permitted to do

rude (*adj*) opposite of *polite*

rocket (*n*) a long thin object that uses hot gasses to move it through space. The motor of a spaceship.

screen (*n*) the part of a television or computer that shows pictures

Solar System (*n*) the Sun and the planets

spacebus (*n*) a small spaceship

spaceship (*n*) a vehicle for travelling great distances in space

speed (*n*) velocity. The car travelled at a *speed* of 80 kilometres per hour.

speed of light (*n*) one thousand million kilometres per hour, nothing can go faster than the *speed of light*.

stairs (*n*) steps for going up or down, from one floor to another floor

supermassive (*adj*) very big and heavy, something which has a lot of mass

supernova (*n*) an exploding star

surface (*n*) the exterior or top part of something

surfing (*n*) the sport of riding waves

towel (*n*) a piece of cloth for drying yourself

truth (*n*) something which is true

wave (*n*) a vibration, an up and down movement. The *waves* in the sea move up and down.

weigh (*v*) to measure how heavy something is

weightless (*adj*) if you are *weightless*, you do not weigh anything

wormhole (*n*) a tunnel or hole in space and time